From DNA to GM Wheat

Discovering Genetic Modification of Food

John Farndon

Heinemann
LIBRARY

www.heinemann.co.uk/library
Visit our website to find out more information about Heinemann Library books.

To order:
📞 Phone 44 (0) 1865 888066
📄 Send a fax to 44 (0) 1865 314091
💻 Visit the Heinemann Bookshop at www.heinemann.co.uk/library to browse
our catalogue and order online.

Produced for Heinemann Library by
White-Thomson Publishing Ltd,
Bridgewater Business Centre,
210 High Street,
Lewes, East Sussex BN7 2NH

First published in Great Britain by Heinemann Library,
Jordan Hill, Oxford OX2 8EJ, part of Harcourt Education.
Heinemann Library is a registered trademark of Harcourt
Education Ltd.

Consultant: Michael Reiss
Commissioning editor: Andrew Farrow
Editors: Kelly Davis and Richard Woodham
Proofreader: Catherine Clarke
Design: Tim Mayer
Picture research: Amy Sparks
Artwork: William Donohoe pp. 15, 45, 46;
Wooden Ark pp. 13, 18.

Originated by RMW
Printed and bound in China by South China
Printing Company

10 digit ISBN 0431185956 (hardback)
13 digit ISBN 978-0-431-18595-8 (hardback)
11 10 09 08 07
10 9 8 7 6 5 4 3 2 1

British Library Cataloguing in Publication Data
Farndon, John
From DNA to GM Wheat - discovering genetic
modification of food. - (Chain reactions)
631.5'233
A full catalogue record for this book is available from the
British Library.

Acknowledgements. The author and publisher would like
to thank the following for allowing their pictures to be
reproduced in this publication:

Corbis pp. 4–5 (Jim Richardson), 17 (Andrew Brookes),
21 (Bettmann), 34 (Steve Kaufman), 53 (Caroline Penn),
54–55 (Reuters/Jean-Philippe Arles); Index Stock
Imagery pp. 14 (Photolibrary), 36, 38, 47; Marshall
University, College of Science, West Virginia, USA
p. 27; Science Photo Library pp. 1 (David Aubrey), 6
(BSIP VEM), 8 (Gary Gaugler), 9 (Dr. Gopal Murti), 10,
11, 12 (Lynette Cook), 16 (National Library of Medicine),
19 (Professor Stanley Cohen), 20 (Martin Riedl), 22
(Will and Deni McIntyre), 23 (Maximilian Stock Ltd),
24 (SCIMAT), 25 (Geoff Kidd), 26 (Matt Meadows, Peter
Arnold Inc.), 28 (Susumu Nishinaga), 29 (Simon Fraser),
30 (David Aubrey), 32 (Bill Barksdale/Agstock), 35
(Cordelia Molloy), 40 (TH Foto-Werbung), 48 (Ph.
Plailly/Eurelios), 49 (AJ Photo), 50 (Simon Fraser),
cover (Adam Gault); Topfoto.co.uk pp. 7 (Richard
Lord/The Image Works), 41 (Sean Sprague/The Image
Works), 42 (Michael Schwarz/The Image Works), 44
(Photri), 52 (Sean Sprague/The Image Works).

Cover design by Tim Mayer.

Contents

Any words appearing in the text in bold, **like this**, are explained in the Glossary.

Marvellous foods or dangerous developments?

Did you know that farmers may one day grow chocolate-flavoured strawberries? Or tomatoes that never rot? Or that the milk from goats could be used to make bulletproof vests? These are examples of genetically modified (GM) food and farm products. All these developments stem from the discovery of **DNA**.

DNA is a very special chemical. All living things are built from microscopic packages called cells. There are tiny bundles of DNA in the middle of every single cell. These bundles are far too small to see, except under the most powerful microscopes. But each one is a complete plan for life.

DNA is made up of thousands of **genes**. Genes are every living thing's instructions for life, passed on from one generation to the next. Genes tell your body how to grow. They also tell it how to create an entirely new human being, which is what happens when a mother has a baby.

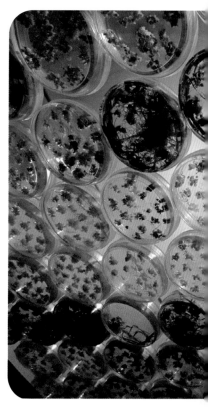

? WHEN DID FOOD MODIFICATION FIRST START?

Scientific gene modification is new, but farmers have modified genes for food crops in their own way for thousands of years. The corn we see growing in fields today, for instance, is very different from corn in ancient times. Corn was originally a type of small wild grass. But, over 10,000 years, farmers carefully selected which seeds to plant. By planting only the seeds that gave the biggest, best corn, they gradually modified corn and changed it into the plant we see today.

The beginning of genetic modification

The discovery of the structure of DNA in 1953 triggered an amazing series of scientific advances. Within 15 years, scientists found that they could move genes from one living thing to another. This is called genetic modification (GM for short). Now genetic modification is leading to all kinds of GM crops and food: corn plants that kill pests, potatoes with added vitamins, and many more besides.

Some people believe that genetic modification will give us many marvellous foods and help us feed the world's poor. But others argue that changing genes could have terrible, unforeseen effects on wildlife – and maybe even on the people who eat GM food. Whatever the truth, the story is a fascinating one.

A researcher at Cornell University, in the United States, examines genetically modified rice plants. New types of GM crops are being developed all the time.

THAT'S AMAZING!

In the future, foods may be genetically modified so much that they will be barely recognizable. For example, animal cells could be grown into chunks of meat in a laboratory. These chunks of meat might be grown in seawater and fed by sunlight alone! That way, vast areas of the world's oceans could be turned into food factories.

Discovering DNA

The story of genetically modified food began in 1869 when a young Swiss biology student, called Friedrich Miescher (1844–1895), discovered the chemical now known as **DNA**.

WHAT ARE ATOMS AND MOLECULES?

Everything in the universe is made up of atoms. Each **element** is made from a different-sized atom. Atoms rarely occur by themselves. Instead, they join together in standard groups called **molecules**.

A water molecule is made up of two hydrogen atoms and one oxygen atom. In this computer illustration of a water molecule, the red sphere represents an oxygen atom, and the green spheres represent hydrogen atoms.

By the mid-1800s, biologists knew that all living things were made of tiny packages called cells – usually too small to see with the naked eye. They also knew that cells were made of fats, sugars, **proteins**, and **nucleic acids**. Nucleic acids are chemicals that sit in the **nucleus**, in the centre of every cell.

A cell's nucleus is extremely small, so studying nucleic acids was very tricky. Yet that was what Miescher decided to do when he was a student in Germany. His idea was to collect old blood-soaked bandages. The pus on the bandages was rich in **white blood cells**. White blood cells have a big nucleus. Under his microscope, Miescher could see tiny knots in each nucleus. He called these knots "nuclein". His tutor, Ernst Hoppe-Seyler, investigated and found that they were acidic. Later, nuclein came to be called nucleic acid, then deoxyribonucleic acid, or DNA.

Miescher's guess

Miescher studied nuclein all his life. In the 1870s, he extracted pure DNA from the big sperm cells of salmon he caught in rivers in the Alps. He later showed that there was DNA in the nucleus of every living cell.

Miescher knew that DNA was a molecule, the smallest possible piece of a particular chemical. He also knew that it was linked to **heredity**, which is the way living things pass on their characteristics to their offspring. Like every molecule, DNA is made up of atoms. Miescher wondered if DNA controlled heredity through the way its atoms were arranged. Much later, other scientists found that he was right, and used his discovery to investigate genetics.

Three generations of a family look at photographs at their home in the United States. They share a family resemblance, passed down through their **genes**.

WHAT IS HEREDITY?

Every plant and animal resembles not only its parents but also its grandparents, great-grandparents, and so on. This is called heredity. Family characteristics are passed on, but with subtle variations each time. These subtle differences allow each **species** (type of living thing) to change and develop. For instance, giraffes gradually developed longer necks, because those with long necks could reach leaves high in trees, and so had a better chance of survival.

Finding out what DNA does

For almost 80 years after Miescher discovered **DNA**, nobody paid it much attention. Then, in the 1940s, scientists studying pneumonia **bacteria** made an amazing discovery.

This is a photograph of *Streptococcus pneumoniae* bacteria, magnified about 13,000 times.

Many diseases are caused by bacteria. Pneumonia is caused by a bacterium called *Streptococcus pneumoniae*. There are two different **strains** of this bacterium. One strain looks smooth under a microscope. The other looks rough. Yet only the S (smooth) strain is dangerous. The R (rough) strain is harmless.

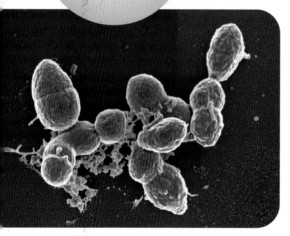

In 1928, a British scientist called Frederick Griffith (1881–1941) was experimenting with pneumonia bacteria when he found something strange. If he injected mice with the harmless R strain, the mice survived. If he killed the S strain by heating it, then injected the mice with the dead S strain, the mice survived. But if he injected the mice with both the R strain and the dead S strain, they died. The R bacteria were getting something from the dead S bacteria that made them dangerous. This substance was changing the R bacteria's life instructions.

THAT'S AMAZING!

There are an estimated 5 trillion quadrillion quadrillion bacteria on Earth. That's a 5 with 42 zeros after it! Together, they weigh more than all the plants in the world. There are thousands of different bacteria **species**. Some are germs that cause disease, but most are completely harmless. In fact, each square centimetre of your skin has about 100,000 bacteria living on it without doing you any harm.

The DNA in a cell **nucleus** is mixed with **protein**. The DNA and protein make threads called **chromosomes**. Chromosomes usually come in pairs. Humans have 23 pairs. In 22 of the pairs, the chromosomes match each other exactly. Only the 23rd pair of chromosomes, which carry information about sex, may be different. When cells divide to multiply, one half of each pair of chromosomes goes to each cell. Each chromosome is then copied to form a new pair in the new cell.

What makes bacteria dangerous?

In the 1940s, a Canadian scientist called Oswald Avery (1877–1955) and his team were working in New York, in the United States. They decided to find out what changed the R bacteria's life instructions. They destroyed each bit of the S bacteria in turn, in order to track down the culprit.

nucleus

Even with various bits destroyed, the S strain went on making the R bacteria dangerous. Then, finally, Avery destroyed the S strain's DNA. At once the R bacteria stayed safe. Clearly, it was the S strain's DNA that transformed the R bacteria's life instructions. Now scientists all over the world became very interested in DNA. Could DNA be involved in the life instructions of all living things?

This photograph shows a human kidney cell dividing, magnified about 1,800 times. The nucleus has divided in two. The two daughter cells will soon separate entirely, each one containing identical genetic material.

Working out the structure of DNA

By the 1950s, scientists knew it was DNA that gave living things their instructions for living and growing. But they did not know just how it did so. Might it be something to do with the actual shape of the DNA **molecule**?

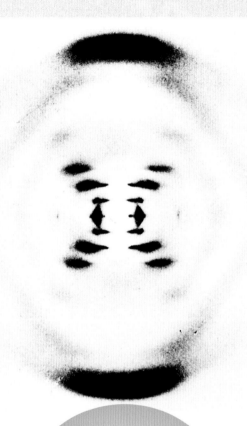

This photograph of DNA was taken by Rosalind Franklin in 1953. To take it, she shone X-rays through a DNA molecule. The DNA molecule scattered the rays into a pattern of spots and bands. This pattern revealed the spiral structure of the molecule.

Scientists had known for a long time that DNA was made up of three main ingredients: a kind of sugar called ribose, some **phosphates**, and some chemicals called **bases**. In the 1930s, they found that DNA was a very long, thin, thread-like molecule. Now they needed to find out just how the sugars, phosphates, and bases were arranged.

Scientists around the world raced to see who could find out first. The first to come up with an idea was American scientist Linus Pauling (1901–1994). Pauling suggested that the DNA molecule was a spiral, or helix. He imagined a long, twisted thread of sugars and phosphates, with spines of bases coming off, like the legs on a millipede. But scientists knew that DNA was an acid, and that no molecule this shape could be an acid. Pauling could not be right.

Double the spiral

In 1952, a young woman called Rosalind Franklin (1920–1958) was working at King's College, London. Her approach was to photograph DNA using X-rays. She was determined to see the structure for herself, rather than working it out theoretically as Pauling and others were doing.

James Watson (left) and Francis Crick (right) are shown here with their model of part of a DNA molecule in 1953.

A young American, James Watson, and an Englishman, called Francis Crick (1916–2004), were also working on the DNA problem at the Cavendish Laboratory in Cambridge, in the United Kingdom. When they saw Rosalind Franklin's photographs, they became convinced that DNA was a spiral shape. They began to build rough models.

Finally, in February 1953, Watson and Crick made their breakthrough. They realized that the DNA molecule must be two parallel twisted chains, not one. It was made from two thin strands wrapped tightly around each other in a double helix or spiral. It looked rather like a twisted rope ladder. The "ropes" were made of sugars and phosphates. The "rungs" were chemicals called bases, linked together by hydrogen bonds.

TALKING SCIENCE

"It was quite a moment. We felt sure that this was it. Anything that simple, that elegant just had to be right. [...] If you knew the sequence – the order of bases – along one chain, you automatically knew the sequence along the other. It was immediately apparent that this must be how the genetic messages of genes are copied so exactly..."
James Watson, *DNA: The Secret of Life* (William Heinemann, 2003)

This is an artist's impression of Earth about 3.5 billion years ago. Life may have begun at this time, when complex organic chemicals joined by chance into RNA, a chemical that could copy itself.

Finding the messenger molecule: RNA

Once scientists knew DNA's shape, they wanted to know how it worked. By the late 1950s, they knew that DNA tells cells to make proteins. Proteins are needed to make everything, from cell walls to muscles. One important kind of protein is an **enzyme**. Enzymes are helper chemicals that get chemical processes going. Without them, living things would not function.

Scientists wanted to know exactly how DNA tells a cell to make proteins. They were certain that the chemical bases along each strand of DNA were involved. The order in which the bases were arranged seemed to act like a code or recipe.

At first, scientists thought that DNA simply exposed a segment with the right "recipe" of bases. The ingredients would then come together to make a particular protein, almost like making a cake. Then scientists discovered that another chemical, called **RNA**, played a part in the process.

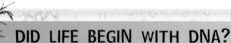

DID LIFE BEGIN WITH DNA?

Scientists once thought that life began with DNA. Yet DNA can only copy itself if there are proteins around. Likewise, proteins can only be made with DNA, so how did the first DNA get made? This question puzzled scientists until they realized that life did not start with DNA, but with RNA. RNA can copy itself without any proteins. RNA was therefore the first life chemical. But it was rather unstable. This is why life only got going when DNA was made from RNA.

While DNA is rather like a computer's hard drive, RNA is more like a temporary file. DNA sits in the cell's nucleus all the time, as a permanent data store. Meanwhile, RNA moves around the whole cell, giving instructions. Before long, scientists knew that DNA controls life by telling RNA to make proteins.

How do DNA and RNA work together?

DNA is too valuable for the cell to use directly to make proteins. It would soon get worn out. When the cell needs a new protein, the cell sends a special enzyme into the nucleus. The enzyme triggers the DNA to copy the right section of code on to a piece of RNA. The copying process is called transcription, and the copies are called messenger RNA or mRNA.

The copied mRNA drifts out to the cell's **ribosomes** (protein-making units). Meanwhile, chemicals called **amino acids** are brought to the ribosomes by short strands of another kind of RNA, called transfer RNA or tRNA. The mRNA runs through the ribosomes, hooking in the right amino acids, using matching strands of tRNA. For example, tRNA carrying the amino acid lysine might only bind to the bases AAA. As it does this, the amino acids are strung together to make the protein.

This diagram shows how tRNA brings amino acids to the ribosome, to be assembled into proteins by mRNA.

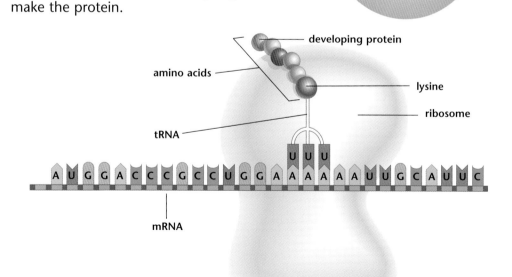

developing protein

amino acids

lysine

ribosome

tRNA

U U U

A U G G A C C C G C C U G G A A A A A A U U G C A U U C

mRNA

Breaking the DNA code

Scientists now knew that **DNA**'s instructions to make **proteins** come in the sequence of chemicals along its length. They also realized that this sequence of chemicals acts like a code. But just how did this code work?

At the centre of the search were DNA's **bases**, the chemicals that formed the rungs of the **molecule's** "rope ladder". There are four bases: adenine (A), guanine (G), thymine (T), and cytosine (C). It is the order in which these four bases are arranged that gives the code.

In 1961, Francis Crick and Sidney Brenner took the first big step towards breaking the code. They conducted a series of experiments at Cambridge University, in the United Kingdom. In these experiments, they showed that the four bases are arranged in groups of three. Each group of three bases (known as a **codon**) codes for a particular **amino acid**. A single codon codes for a single amino acid. A sequence of codons codes for all the amino acids needed to make a particular protein.

WHAT ARE ESSENTIAL AMINO ACIDS?

All proteins are made up of different combinations of basic chemicals called amino acids. There are 20 amino acids. The human body can make 12 of these acids itself, but it needs to get the others from food. Without the amino acids from food, the body cannot build all the proteins it needs. This is why the acids we get from food are called essential amino acids.

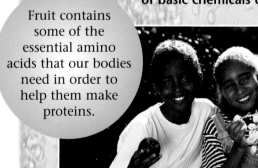

Fruit contains some of the essential amino acids that our bodies need in order to help them make proteins.

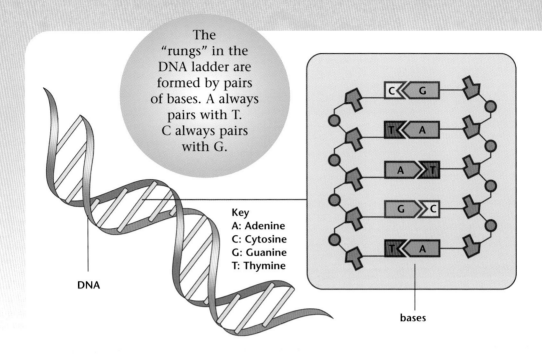

The "rungs" in the DNA ladder are formed by pairs of bases. A always pairs with T. C always pairs with G.

Key
A: Adenine
C: Cytosine
G: Guanine
T: Thymine

DNA

bases

There are 64 ways in which the 4 bases can be arranged in groups of 3. This means there are 64 different codons. Yet there are only 20 amino acids. This means that some amino acids must be coded for by several different codons. Scientists also found that three of the codons simply act like full stops, ending the code for a particular protein.

The codons for each acid

Later the same year, a young American biochemist called Marshall Nirenberg took the second big step towards breaking the code. He discovered the combination of bases that coded for a particular amino acid, called phenylalanine. Over the next five years, Nirenberg and two other scientists, Gobind Khorana and Robert Holley, worked through each of the 64 codons, finding out which acid each one coded for. By 1966, they had worked out the entire **genetic code**. For this brilliant work, the scientists received a Nobel Prize in 1968.

The mechanics of DNA

Once scientists understood how the **DNA** code worked, they began to wonder if they could change it. If they could change the code, they could alter **genes**, and so life itself. First, though, they had to learn a bit more about the mechanics of DNA.

Arthur Kornberg, American biochemist and Nobel Prize winner, is seen here in his laboratory.

To grow or reproduce, an **organism's** cells split in two. When a cell splits in two, its DNA is copied, and one copy goes to each of the new cells. The two strands of the parent cell's DNA (the two sides of the "rope ladder") temporarily split apart. Each strand is used to make a copy. The copies then join together to make a new DNA **molecule**, which is identical to the original. This is called **replication**.

In the 1950s, American scientist Arthur Kornberg discovered that a certain **enzyme** plays a key part in replication. This enzyme is called DNA polymerase. Using DNA polymerase, Kornberg artificially replicated the DNA of a **virus**. Scientists could see no difference between Kornberg's copied DNA and the original. Yet, for some reason, his artificial copy did not work. Then, in 1967, scientists found out why: it needed a chemical called ligase.

Ligase is DNA's "glue". Using ligase, Kornberg could join the ends of his copied DNA together in a loop, like the original. Immediately, the DNA started to work.

"Biological scissors"

At about the same time, Swiss scientist Werner Arber made another important discovery about DNA. This discovery was the role played by **proteins** called restriction enzymes. Restriction enzymes are chemicals that cells use to protect themselves against any foreign DNA that gets in. These enzymes simply cut through the invading DNA and stop it working. Arber realized that scientists could use restriction enzymes like "biological scissors" to cut DNA.

Now that scientists had restriction enzymes, they could snip through DNA to get at particular sections. With ligase, they could glue sections into place. If you think of DNA as if it were a computer file, they could "cut" with restriction enzymes and "paste" with ligase.

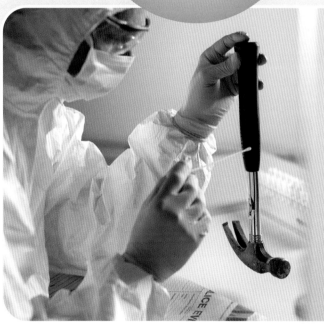

This forensic scientist is looking for DNA in the form of blood or hair. The tiniest fragment of DNA, found in a drop of dried blood or a single hair root, can be expanded into a sufficient quantity to be tested.

THAT'S AMAZING!

The discovery of DNA polymerase led to an extraordinary invention: DNA fingerprinting. Each person's DNA is unique, rather like a fingerprint. This uniqueness is very useful to the police when they are investigating crimes. For instance, if a drop of blood is left at the crime scene, the DNA in the blood can be compared to the DNA of a suspected criminal. There is actually very little DNA in dried blood. But scientists can use a technique called Polymerase Chain Reaction (PCR) to expand the DNA by getting it to multiply. This gives them a big enough sample to study properly.

Learning more about copying DNA

By the late 1960s, scientists could cut DNA strands with restriction enzymes and paste them together with ligase. The next vital step came in 1971, when they learned more about how to copy and transfer bits of DNA.

This breakthrough depended on a strange discovery about **bacteria**. In the 1960s, scientists were researching why disease-causing bacteria often gained resistance to antibiotic drugs. They found that many bacteria had little extra loops of DNA floating around inside them.

This diagram shows how DNA can be transferred using bacteria. DNA taken from the cells of an organism are inserted into plasmid loops taken from bacteria. These modified loops are taken in by some of the bacterial cells.

These extra loops, called **plasmids**, are so tiny that they can easily slip from one bacterial cell to another. As they enter a new cell, they can give it a batch of new DNA information. The researchers found that this new information sometimes included instructions on how to resist antibiotics.

In 1971, an American scientist, Stanley Cohen, found that he could persuade bacteria to take in plasmids he supplied. This was an amazing discovery. Cohen realized that plasmids could work just like a computer CD. A CD lets you transfer data from one computer to another. In a similar way, plasmids can carry strands of DNA data from one cell to another.

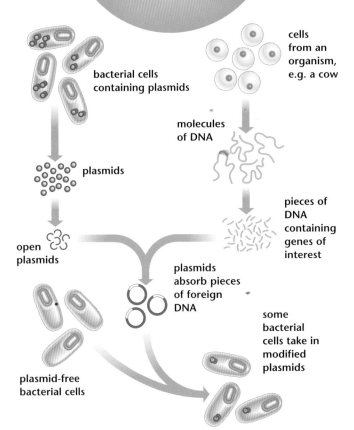

bacterial cells containing plasmids

cells from an organism, e.g. a cow

molecules of DNA

plasmids

pieces of DNA containing genes of interest

open plasmids

plasmids absorb pieces of foreign DNA

some bacterial cells take in modified plasmids

plasmid-free bacterial cells

Altering DNA

Now scientists had all the tools they needed to alter DNA in any way they wished. Altering DNA has become known as genetic modification or **genetic engineering**. In 1972, Cohen teamed up with San Francisco scientist Herbert Boyer and they began to put their knowledge into practice.

Using restriction enzymes, they cut up pieces of plasmid and mixed them together in the same tube. Then they added ligase. The ligase glued the pieces of plasmid together. Sometimes the ligase simply rejoined the plasmids as they were originally. Sometimes, however, the ligase joined different bits of plasmid, combining their DNA. These mixed plasmids are called **recombinant DNA**.

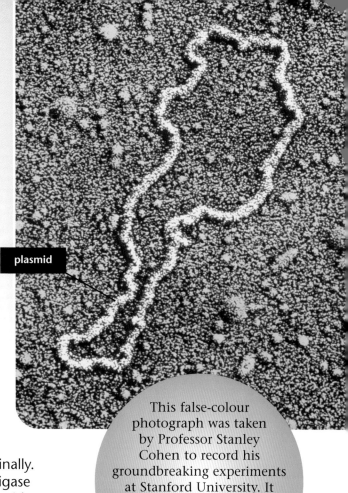

plasmid

This false-colour photograph was taken by Professor Stanley Cohen to record his groundbreaking experiments at Stanford University. It shows a plasmid of bacterial DNA which has been magnified about 70,000 times.

? WHAT WAS THE FIRST GENETICALLY MODIFIED ORGANISM?

Herbert Boyer and Stanley Cohen were very excited by their discovery of the recombinant DNA technique. They decided to try it out immediately. First, they took a piece of DNA from an African clawed toad. Then they used a plasmid to insert this DNA into bacteria. It worked! This was the first example of genetic engineering, and the bacterium was the first genetically modified organism (GMO). From then on, scientists could change the life instructions of living organisms, including food crops, almost as they wished.

Living chemical factories

Scientists were very excited by the discovery that they could alter **genes**. They soon began to wonder just which genes they could alter.

The possibilities were so enormous that numerous biotech companies were set up, such as Genentech and Biogen. These companies poured money into scientific research. It was a risk spending so much. But if they could come up with the right product, they might make a great deal of money.

Competition was fierce, as biotech companies' research labs raced to develop new products. Soon, long court cases were being fought over which idea belonged to whom. Meanwhile, scientists were hard at work in laboratories, especially in the United States and in the United Kingdom.

They wanted to identify genes for useful **proteins**. At first, they looked for proteins that were important for medical treatment. There would be a great demand for these proteins, which could lead to big profits.

One idea was to make human insulin. Insulin is a **hormone** that controls blood sugar level. Diabetics become ill because their bodies do not make insulin properly. They can be treated with injections of insulin taken from pigs. But scientists felt that giving them human insulin, made by genetically modified (GM) **bacteria**, might be more effective. There are 20 million diabetics in the United States alone, so there was a huge market for such a product.

This schoolgirl is being injected with insulin. Diabetics have to follow a strict diet and use daily insulin injections to maintain their blood sugar level.

Biotech companies competed to be the first to make human insulin. They used a bacterium called *Escherichia coli* (E. coli for short). They planned to introduce the gene for human insulin into the bacteria, then get the modified bacteria to multiply in a huge vat. As the bacteria multiplied, they would follow their genes' instructions and make a lot of human insulin. The race was won by Genentech, a US company, in 1978. Their human insulin was the first GM product on the market.

WHAT WAS THE "PANDORA'S BOX CONFERENCE"?

Some scientists were very worried about transferring genes. What if GM bacteria began to multiply and spread? They said it was like "opening Pandora's box". They were referring to the Greek legend of a young woman whose curiosity led her to open a box and let out all the evils, such as war and disease, that cause human suffering. In February 1975, 140 scientists gathered in California, in the United States, to discuss what to do. This meeting became known as "the Pandora's Box Conference". The delegates decided that scientists should never use disease-causing bacteria. In addition, any GM bacteria should only be handled in a secure room, where there was no chance of them escaping.

This illustration of Pandora opening the box is by Walter Crane.

New drugs

As profits from sales of human insulin poured in, biotech companies began to consider modifying bacteria to make other proteins. Another area of research was human growth hormone (HGH).

HGH is a chemical that is vital for proper growth. Children who lack HGH often fail to grow properly. Doctors had been treating children with HGH taken from corpses. Unfortunately, this put the children at risk of infection with Creutzfeld-Jakob disease. In 1982, Genentech scientists managed to modify E. coli bacteria to make HGH. Their genetically modified HGH went on sale in 1985.

Another important protein that scientists succeeded in making with GM bacteria was erythropoetin (EPO). This protein stimulates the body to make red blood cells. It is vital for patients undergoing treatment for kidney disease. When the biotech company Amgen made a GM version of EPO, it proved to be very successful. It has earned the company about US$2 billion every year since its launch.

Soon insulin, HGH, EPO, and various other proteins could all be made by GM bacteria. Once they had learned how to make all these proteins, the biotech companies began to look for other proteins that they could make using genetic modification.

This 11-year-old boy, who is undergoing treatment with human growth hormone, is being measured by his doctor.

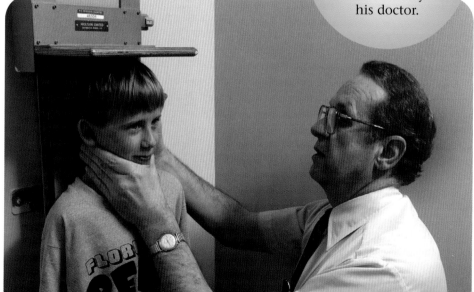

Pharmaceutical technicians in Germany work at a row of fermentation vats. The bacteria in the vats have been **genetically engineered** to produce proteins for use in drugs.

One promising area seemed to be monoclonal **antibodies**. Antibodies are proteins that the body uses to identify and destroy germs. Monoclonal antibodies (MAbs) are antibodies that are completely identical, because they are all perfect copies of the original. Scientists hoped that they could make MAbs target particular cells with pinpoint accuracy. If so, they could perhaps be used to treat cancer.

Biotech companies poured money into research on MAbs in the 1980s, but the results were quite disappointing. However, in recent years, several MAb drugs have been created. These include Herceptin, a drug made by Genentech to treat breast cancer, and ReoPro, a drug made by Centocor to reduce the risk of blood clots in heart patients.

GENENTECH'S STORY

Genentech was the world's first biotech company. It was founded in April 1976 by financier Robert Swanson with scientist Herbert Boyer, who pioneered **recombinant DNA** with Stanley Cohen. They wanted to find a way to use recombinant DNA to make proteins they could sell, such as human insulin. They planned to insert the gene for such a protein into bacteria. Once the bacteria had made the protein in the laboratory, Genentech would start large-scale factory production.

Engineering crops

By the mid-1970s, scientists had all the skills they needed to engineer **genes** and insert them into **bacteria**. But what if they could get engineered genes into plants?

Farmers have always tried to improve their crops. They might select seeds from only the tallest plants, for instance. Or they might combine the qualities of two plants by placing the **pollen** of one on the seeds of the other. **Genetic engineering** opened up some dramatic new possibilities.

There were problems to overcome, however. To alter bacteria genes, scientists put the altered genes in **plasmids**. The plasmids are then taken in by the bacteria. Once they are in the bacteria, the plasmid genes become part of the bacteria's own **DNA**. This means that all the bacteria's offspring include the modified genes. Only bacteria have plasmids, though. To alter crop genes, scientists had to find another way of getting altered genes into plant cells.

Getting genes into plants

The answer actually turned out to be bacteria. *Agrobacterium tumefaciens* is a bacterium that lives in soil.

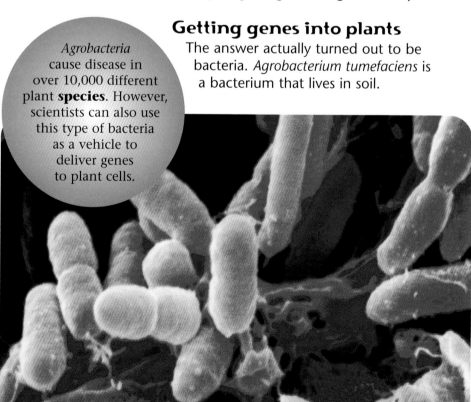

Agrobacteria cause disease in over 10,000 different plant **species**. However, scientists can also use this type of bacteria as a vehicle to deliver genes to plant cells.

Whenever a plant is damaged, *Agrobacteria* can get inside it. They then feed on chemicals released by the plant cells. What makes the bacteria special is the way they make the plant cells multiply by sneaking some of their DNA into the **nuclei** of plant cells. As the plant cells multiply, they make more of the chemicals that the bacteria feed on. Scientists wondered if *Agrobacteria* could be used to sneak engineered genes into crop plants.

First, the scientists inactivated the genes that *Agrobacteria* sneaked into the plant. This meant that the *Agrobacteria* could not harm the plant. Then they replaced the inactivated genes with their own engineered plant genes. In this way, they could get the *Agrobacteria* to sneak the engineered genes into the plant cells. Plants could now be genetically engineered.

This round growth, known as a crown gall, is caused by *Agrobacteria*.

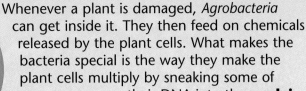

HOW DO BACTERIA GET THEIR DNA INTO PLANTS?

When a plant is damaged, *Agrobacteria* can get into the plant through the wound. Inside the plant, the bacteria make a tunnel into the plant cells, and send a package of their DNA (called tDNA) into each cell. The tDNA is then taken in by the plant cells' own DNA. The tDNA tells the cells to make growth hormone, a chemical that stimulates a cancer-like cell growth. The plant cells then multiply rapidly, producing a large growth called a **gall**. The bacteria feed on the extra **amino acids** that these new cells produce. However, the gall can kill young, tender plants.

The gene gun

Scientists first used *Agrobacteria* to get engineered genes into plant cells. However, this technique only works for a few crops, such as tobacco. At first, it would not work for many major food crops, such as wheat, rice, and maize. Because of this, scientists looked for other ways to insert their engineered genes into plants.

The most successful method was developed in the 1980s. The scientist who discovered it was John Sanford, who was at Cornell University, in the United States. His technique was so violent that it soon became known as the "shotgun method".

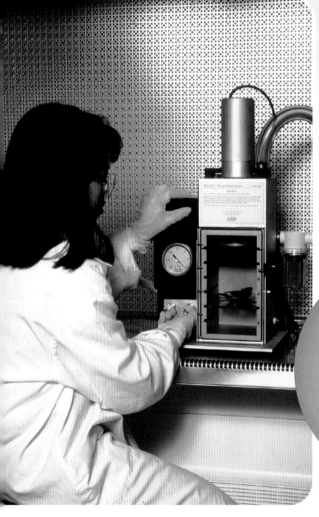

This technician is adjusting the controls on a gene gun. The gun shoots microscopic DNA-coated gold pellets on to the plant leaves in the chamber. The DNA enters the plant cell's nucleus, giving the cell new characteristics.

TALKING SCIENCE

When developing his gene gun, John Sanford experimented with onions because they have particularly large cells. He often joked that the combination of blasted onions and gunpowder made his laboratory smell like *"a McDonald's on a firing range"*!

Sanford's technique involved mixing the engineered DNA with microscopic balls of gold or tungsten metal, rather like tiny shotgun pellets. The DNA stuck to the pellets. The DNA-coated pellets were then placed in front of a blast of gunpowder or pressurized gas. The blast fired the pellets into a plant. The trick was to fire the pellets with enough force to enter the plant's cells, but not so much that they were blown out through the other side.

Many of the plant's cells were destroyed by the blast. But even if only a few pellets lodged inside live cells, this was enough. The cell repaired itself, and took the engineered DNA into its own genes. From these modified cells, a plant could in time be grown with all the engineered characteristics.

By 1987, Sanford had created a neat, hand-held gene gun for firing engineered genes. Within a few years, scientists were using the gun to fire new genes into corn.

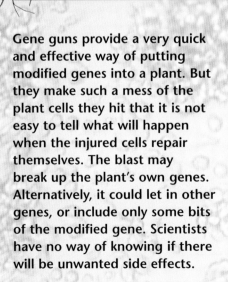

? WHAT ARE THE DISADVANTAGES OF GENE GUNS?

This photograph shows how a gene gun is used to fire genes into plants.

Gene guns provide a very quick and effective way of putting modified genes into a plant. But they make such a mess of the plant cells they hit that it is not easy to tell what will happen when the injured cells repair themselves. The blast may break up the plant's own genes. Alternatively, it could let in other genes, or include only some bits of the modified gene. Scientists have no way of knowing if there will be unwanted side effects.

Electroporation

Scientists still wanted to find other ways to get their engineered genes into crops. *Agrobacteria* worked very well, but only for a few plants. Gene guns worked for many more, but often damaged the plant. Then, in 1990, scientists thought of a third technique. The idea was to use electricity to push engineered genes through the **pores** of plant **pollen**. This is called **electroporation**.

Electroporation was discovered by two scientists working for the US Government Farms Department, James Saunders and Benjamin Matthews. It involves a number of steps:

1. Saunders and Matthews took a gene from E. coli bacteria, which can be found in the human stomach.

2. Then they took grains of pollen from a tobacco plant.

3. They put the pollen in a **culture** (a dish filled with the right nutrients to encourage the pollen to **germinate**).

4. Soon the pollen germinated and grew tiny tubes in order to insert its genes into the female egg cell.

These sunflower pollen grains have been magnified about 2,100 times. Their spiky coating helps them stick to pollinating insects.

5. Immediately, Saunders and Matthews mixed their bacteria gene into the pollen culture.

6. Then they zapped the culture with electricity. The electricity made tiny pores open in the pollen tubes.

7. The pores stayed open for about half an hour. In that time, the bacteria gene slipped in.

8. Once inside, it was taken in by the pollen's DNA.

9. Finally, the scientists put the modified pollen on the female parts of a tobacco plant. The tobacco plant would then grow with the bacteria gene.

WHAT IS POLLEN?

Most plants have male and female parts for making seeds. Pollen is the name for the microscopic grains made by the male parts of a plant, called **stamens**. For new seeds to develop, pollen must land on the plant's female part, called a **stigma**. The stigma contains the eggs, from which seeds will grow. When pollen lands on the stigma, the pollen germinates. This means that the pollen grains grow tiny tubes that allow them to insert their genes into the egg.

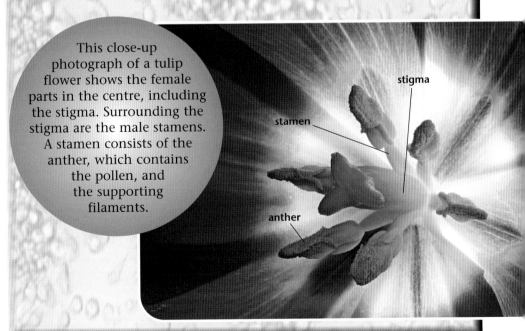

This close-up photograph of a tulip flower shows the female parts in the centre, including the stigma. Surrounding the stigma are the male stamens. A stamen consists of the anther, which contains the pollen, and the supporting filaments.

stigma

stamen

anther

Producing tough plants

Once scientists knew how to get **genes** into crop plants, they searched for genes to insert. They started with genes that help plants fight pests or survive in tough conditions, such as cold or drought.

Pesticide-resistant plants

Many farmers are affected by pests that eat their crops. Insect **larvae**, which feed on plant leaves, are particularly troublesome. For this reason, scientists began to look for genes that might help crops resist insect pests. Their search focused on **bacteria** called *Bacillus thuringiensis* (Bt for short).

Bt was first identified in 1901 as the germ that devastated Japan's silkworms. Silkworms are the larvae (caterpillars) of silk moths. In Japan, the Bt germ got into the silkworms' stomachs and released a toxin. This toxin killed the silkworms. Scientists soon discovered that the Bt toxin could kill other insect pests in the same way. Yet it was completely harmless to humans and other animals. By 1938, Bt toxin had been made into a **pesticide** to spray over crops.

The caterpillars of the Monarch butterfly only eat milkweed leaves. If the milkweed plants are contaminated by pollen from Bt crops, many of the caterpillars could die.

However, the Bt pesticide spray had to be used in huge quantities. This cost farmers a lot of time and money. It also killed insects that were doing no harm to the crops. Scientists from a US company called Monsanto located the gene for the Bt toxin in the Bt bacteria's **DNA**. They then implanted the Bt toxin gene in plant cells, using *Agrobacteria* and gene guns (see page 27). By 1994, they had produced plants with the Bt toxin gene in their own DNA.

Monsanto began producing Bt cotton plants in 1994. Cotton is often attacked by insect larvae called cotton bollworms. Any bollworm trying to eat a Bt cotton plant was in for a fatal meal. Bt cotton quickly became popular in the United States. It is now widely planted in other countries, such as China. Bt cotton has since been joined by Bt soya, Bt corn, Bt potatoes, and several other Bt crops.

ARE GM CROPS A THREAT TO THE MONARCH BUTTERFLY?

The Monarch butterfly is famous for its annual 4,800-kilometre (3,000-mile) migration between central Mexico and the United States. The Monarch caterpillars feed on milkweed leaves. In 1999, some laboratory tests were carried out. **Pollen** from Bt corn was dusted on the milkweed leaves that the caterpillars feed on. Half the caterpillars died in just four days. Some people began to worry that pollen from Bt crops could spread in the air, with disastrous consequences for insect life.

Biotech companies wanted to persuade people that GM crops were good. They argued that planting Bt crops would mean that farmers could use less pesticide. If less pesticide were needed, this would be good for wildlife. This seemed to be true for a while. For a few years, farmers growing Bt crops used half as much pesticide. However, insect pests gradually built up resistance to Bt toxins. Some of these farmers now have to use more pesticide after all.

Weedkiller resistance

Weeds grow among crops and compete with them. This makes it harder to kill weeds than insect pests. Chemicals that kill all weeds could well damage the crops as well. This is why many farmers attack weeds with several different weedkillers, each one effective against a narrow range of plants. This is time-consuming and expensive.

The world's biggest-selling weedkiller, Roundup®, is made by Monsanto. Roundup® is based on a chemical called glyophosphate. It is harmless to animals, but kills nearly all plants. Farmers realized that they had to use it very carefully. If they were careless, Roundup® might kill their crops as well as the weeds.

This photograph, taken in Arkansas, in the United States, shows a genetically modified soya bean crop being sprayed with Roundup®.

In the early 1990s, scientists around the world began to look for a gene that would resist Roundup®. This gene could be inserted into crops. Then the crops could be sprayed freely with Roundup®. All the weeds would be killed, but the crops with the resistant gene would survive.

Monsanto's scientists led the search. The company wanted to sell farmers both Roundup®, to kill all weeds, and special crop seeds with a gene that would enable the crops to resist the weedkiller. These seeds would be known as "Roundup Ready®" seeds.

A small Californian company, called Calgene, found the Roundup Ready® gene in 1992. Calgene's researchers looked for bacteria that were growing in glyophosphate chemical dumps. If these bacteria could grow in glyophosphate dumps, they would clearly be able to resist Roundup® weedkiller.

Roundup Ready® soya beans were first planted in the United States in 1996. Within a year, about 16 per cent of the US soya crop was Roundup Ready®. Soya was soon followed by Roundup Ready® cotton, corn, alfalfa, and wheat. Since then, other companies have developed crops engineered to resist weedkillers in the same way.

COULD GM CROPS LEAD TO "SUPERWEEDS"?

One of the fears about giving crops genes to resist weedkillers was that the genes could spread to weeds. If the genes got into weeds, they could become "superweeds" that are resistant to weedkillers. Although no such weeds have yet appeared, GM genes were found to spread easily between different oilseed rape plants in Canada. GM crops planted in separate fields, with different genes, got the genes from their neighbours within a few years.

Some campaigners believe the only way to ensure that GM genes do not spread is to have a 5-kilometre (3-mile) wide exclusion zone around GM farms. No similar plants can be grown within this zone. This might be possible in large countries such as Canada, but it is impossible in countries such as the United Kingdom where farms in crop-growing areas are not big enough to allow for such large exclusion zones.

Surviving on the edge

In many parts of the world, crops are difficult to grow because the weather is too cold or too dry, or the soil is too salty. Scientists wanted to look for genes that would help crops survive in such tough conditions.

The need to develop salt-resistant plants is very pressing. In the hotter parts of the world, there is so little water that a lot of farmland has to be irrigated (watered artificially). Unfortunately, the water often evaporates in the heat, drawing salt up from the soil. Scientists think that around 25 per cent of the world's irrigated farmlands are now so salty that soon crops will no longer grow.

Back in 1985, Eduardo Blumwald of the University of California, in the United States, discovered an interesting **protein** that occurs in many plants. This protein, known as AtNXH1, is called a transporter protein. It serves a very useful purpose. Sodium is one of the two chemicals that make up salt. When salt levels rise too high in a cell, the AtNXH1 protein transports excess sodium away into spaces in the cell called **vacuoles**.

Irrigation hoses feed salt water to potato plants on an experimental farm at Ashalim, Israel.

Fourteen years later, in 1999, Blumwald was studying the genes of a little plant called mouse cress. In his research, he came across the gene that made AtNXH1. Blumwald modified the genes of mouse cress so that it made more AtNXH1. The modified cress was able to survive in much saltier conditions.

Then Blumwald and Canadian scientist Hong-Xia Zhang modified a tomato plant in the same way. This tomato plant could live in conditions 50 times saltier than normal. It could also draw salt out of the soil, thereby reducing the saltiness of the soil it grew in. All the salt went into the plant's leaves, so the tomato fruits tasted the same as any other tomatoes. The scientists hope that, in future, similar plants may be grown in many dry and salty parts of the world.

THAT'S AMAZING!

In the driest parts of Africa, lack of water is a great problem. Scientists have taken inspiration from the resurrection plant (*Selaginella lepidophylla*). This plant looks dead most of the time when the weather is dry. But as soon as it rains the resurrection plant springs back to life. The plant is able to survive because of a sugar called trehalose.

In 2002, scientists in New York and South Korea modified the genes of rice so that it made its own trehalose. Ray Wu, of New York, modified the rice genes so that the trehalose is only made when the rice is deprived of water. Scientists hope that trehalose genes will enable farmers to grow rice in areas that are currently far too dry.

The resurrection plant on the left is in its dry state. The same plant is shown on the right, one day after watering. This plant is found in the deserts of southern North America.

Self-fertilizing grains

One of the main problems facing modern farmers is the need for huge amounts of artificial **fertilizer**. Farmers today may need to use 10 times as much nitrogen fertilizer to get good yields as they did 40 years ago. This is not only expensive. It can also damage the soil and the environment.

Yet not all crops need artificial fertilizers. For instance, plants called **legumes**, which include peas and beans, do not require fertilizers. Legumes have a close relationship with *Rhizobium* **bacteria**.

The *Rhizobium* bacteria live on the legume's roots and form swellings called **nodules**. Both plant and bacteria benefit from this relationship. The bacteria get a home and food, in the form of sugars made by the plant. In return, the bacteria take nitrogen from the air and change it into ammonia. This is called nitrogen fixing. Plants cannot use nitrogen from the air, but they can use it in the form of ammonia. Cereal crops need to have the ammonia added, in the form of nitrogen fertilizers. Legumes have the bacteria to make it for them.

Like all legumes, clover needs no fertilizer. Bacteria living on its roots can supply it with all the nitrogen it needs.

In the 1990s, scientists discovered why *Rhizobium* lives in legume roots and not cereals. Legume roots produce chemicals called **flavonoids**, which attract the bacteria. Cereals also make flavonoids, but not the right ones. For this reason, scientists thought about introducing **genes** for legume flavonoids into cereals. They also wondered if they could alter the genes of the bacteria so that they were attracted by different flavonoids.

This line of research quickly proved fruitful. By 1997, scientists had altered the genes of the bacteria that normally invade peas so that they invaded clover instead. Now they are trying to develop bacteria that will invade cereal crops. If they can succeed in developing this type of bacteria, the cereals will grow nitrogen-fixing nodules on their roots. They will then become self-fertilizing.

In the meantime, scientists have genetically modified one type of *Rhizobium*, the *Sinorhizobium meliloti* (*S. meliloti*) bacterium that lives on legumes. These modified bacteria are even more attracted to legumes and even better at fixing nitrogen than natural bacteria. Such genetically modified bacteria are now widely used in the United States, though some people have expressed concerns about them (see below).

WILL GM CROPS LEAD TO ANTIBIOTIC-RESISTANT GERMS?

Soil contains fungi that make natural antibiotics. Most of the antibiotic drugs we take to fight disease-causing bacteria come from these soil fungi. The bacteria that help legumes fix nitrogen could easily be attacked by natural antibiotics in the soil. To avoid this problem, scientists developing the GM bacteria *S. meliloti* added genes that made these bacteria resistant to natural antibiotics such as streptomycin. Many people are worried about antibiotic-resistant bacteria being spread in the soil. If antibiotic resistance becomes very widespread among bacteria, our antibiotic medicines might no longer fight disease effectively.

Food for all?

Over the next half century, the population of the world is predicted to grow by 3 billion. Yet millions already starve each year, or are made ill by the lack of good food, especially in Africa and Asia. Some scientists believe that GM technology could help feed the world.

Rice is one of the world's **staples**. Many people in Asia and Africa live mostly on rice. In the late 1990s, scientists began to modify rice in order to boost yields. Corn grows much faster than rice, partly because it is better at taking carbon dioxide from the air. This means that it can make more of its own food with the aid of sunlight. In 2000, scientists transferred corn's carbon dioxide uptake **genes** to rice. Experimental crops showed rice yields that were up to 30 per cent higher than normal.

Many poor people in southern Asia, like these Thai farmers, depend almost entirely on rice. Some scientists hope to engineer rice to include the vitamins people need to stay healthy.

Golden rice

At the same time, scientists around the world worked together to produce "golden rice". Golden rice gets its name because it contains genes for beta-carotene, the substance that gives carrots their orange colour. Beta-carotene helps the body make vitamin A. Between 100 and 400 million children around the world suffer from lack of vitamin A. This makes many of them go blind or even die.

Millions of people also suffer from the iron deficiency disease anaemia. Golden rice has therefore been modified to give extra iron in three ways:

1. Fungus genes make an **enzyme** that gets rid of phylate. Phylate is a chemical in rice that stops the body taking in iron.

2. Spinach genes make ferritin. Ferritin makes the rice store more iron.

3. **Bacteria** genes make cysteine, a **protein** that helps the body absorb iron.

There are still many problems with golden rice. One problem is that beta-carotene only helps raise vitamin A levels when people have plenty of fat in their diet. Yet the people who are most lacking vitamin A often have little or no fat in their diet. Most scientists think golden rice is a step in the right direction. But there has been so much opposition that development of golden rice has been put on hold.

? WHAT WAS THE GREEN REVOLUTION?

In the 20th century, harvests improved so dramatically that people called it the Green Revolution. In Asia, for instance, the main grain crop harvests doubled between 1971 and 1976 alone. The Green Revolution was partly made possible by heavy use of **fertilizers** and **pesticides**. Farmers also started using special high-yield varieties of grain seeds called hybrids. Hybrid grains are produced by deliberately adding the **pollen** of one strain of the crop to another, to combine the best qualities of the two. However, farmers have to buy new seeds each year and this is expensive.

Healthier potatoes for India?

In India many people are vegetarian. Their only sources of protein are vegetables, such as lentils, which are expensive. In the early 2000s, scientists in India began working on ways of modifying potatoes to make them richer in protein. Potatoes are usually very cheap.

There was a lot of opposition to GM crops in India. Bt crops (see page 30) have their own built-in pesticides. However, they can kill useful insects as well as pests. Other crops using genes taken from bacteria or animals were not popular because people thought they seemed unnatural.

These farmers in Karnataka, India, are buying hybrid and GM seeds imported from the United States.

IS GM TECHNOLOGY UNFAIR ON POOR FARMERS?

One reason why many people oppose GM food is that much of the technology is in the hands of a few big multinational companies. There is a concern that poor farmers could be forced into buying expensive seeds from these big companies. The same farmers might also have to buy the particular pesticides and weedkillers that work with GM products alone. The multinational companies would then gain enormous power. Small farmers who chose not to co-operate might be forced off their land by the few big farmers who could afford to pay for the GM technology.

The Indian scientists wanted to avoid controversy. They decided to use only protein-enriching genes from other plants. They took their gene from the amaranth plant. The amaranth is a South American plant that is quite similar to the potato. It is sometimes sold in health food stores because it is high in protein. The gene that gives its high protein content is the AmA1 gene.

By 2003, a team of scientists in New Delhi, led by Govindarajan Padmanaben, had succeeded in getting the AmA1 gene into potatoes. The resulting potatoes were much higher in protein than normal potatoes. In 2005, the modified potato underwent trials. The Indian government will eventually decide whether this protein-rich potato can help make the country's children healthier.

Adding nutrients to food in this way is not a new idea. For instance, people have added iodine to salt for decades, to help avoid health problems caused by lack of iodine. Many breakfast cereals also have vitamins added to them. The difference is that food manufacturers add these substances directly. With GM technology, the plant's genes are being modified so that they make their own extra nutrients.

Amaranth is used as a medicinal herb as well as a food.

Seed control

In the past, farmers always saved some seeds from their harvest to plant the following year's crop. They rarely had to buy seeds. This posed a problem for biotech companies. They might spend years developing a new GM seed, but they could only sell it to the farmer once. After that, the farmer could take the seeds from his harvest. He might even give spare seeds to other farmers.

The Monsanto company looked for a solution. In 1998, scientists in the US Department of Agriculture Laboratory in Lubbock, Texas, came up with a clever technique. They altered the chemistry of GM seeds before they were sold. They flipped the genetic switches that made the plant's seeds start growing. The seeds could still be eaten or turned into flour, but they could never be used to grow new plants.

This is a Monsanto chemical plant by the Mississippi River in Louisiana, USA. Some people believe that companies such as Monsanto have too much power over small farmers, who may be forced to buy seeds from them.

Once news of this breakthrough leaked out, many people got very angry. Newspapers called it the "Terminator gene", after the lethal android played by Arnold Schwarzenegger in the *Terminator* films.

Farmers felt the Terminator gene would deny them their basic right to plant their own seeds. People campaigning against poverty argued that poor farmers' lives would be controlled by the big multinational companies. Each year, they would have to go back to the seed providers to buy more seed that they could barely afford.

Environmental activists feared that the Terminator gene could spread into wild plants. If it did this, it might cause an environmental disaster, because wild flowers would be producing useless seeds.

In the face of all this opposition, the governments of many countries banned Terminator seeds. Others launched investigations into their possible effects. Although most of these investigations found no special risk from the seeds, the damage was done. People in many countries became very suspicious of GM crops.

WHAT IS THE "EXORCIST GENE"?

After developing the Terminator gene, scientist Pim Stemmer began working on another idea, which quickly became known as the "Exorcist gene". Stemmer's idea, first suggested in 2002, is to include the Exorcist gene in every GM seed. This gene would allow the GM seed to grow until just before the seeds and fruit were ready to harvest. Then the gene would suddenly eliminate all the GM genes, including itself. The crop would benefit from all the genetic modifications, but the seeds and fruit would be completely GM-free.

This, Stemmer argues, would solve the GM companies' problems with reselling seeds. It would also overcome people's worries about GM food, because the food from GM crops would not contain any GM genes. Stemmer believes that his idea will work. But many tests will have to be carried out before it becomes a reality.

Changing foods

Most GM technology is aimed at making food crops grow better. But it can be used to modify foods in other ways too. In 1994, the Californian biotech company Calgene made a tomato called the Flavr Savr.

Tomatoes are usually picked while they are still green. Once they are ripe, they quickly go soft, so they have a very short shelf life in shops. Calgene scientists knew that tomatoes went soft because of an **enzyme** called polygalacturonase (PG). The PG enzyme is released as the tomato ripens. The Calgene scientists realized that if they could knock out the PG **gene**, they could make the tomato stay firm longer.

The Flavr Savr tomato stayed fresh longer than other tomatoes but it was not a commercial success.

By inserting a back-to-front copy of the PG gene into the tomato's **DNA**, they could neutralize it. Whenever the tomato made **RNA** copies of the PG gene, it would also make copies of the back-to-front gene. The PG RNA would then become entangled with the back-to-front PG RNA. This would stop the PG working. With this modification, the Flavr Savr tomato could be left on the plant until it was ripe. It would still be firm when it reached the shops.

Unfortunately, Calgene had made one fatal error. The strain of tomato they had chosen to modify was not that tasty. Although the Flavr Savr was in wonderful condition when it was sold, it had no flavour to savour! It also bruised easily.

The Flavr Savr was launched in the United States as a scientific breakthrough in a blaze of publicity. It sold well at first. A short time later it was quietly withdrawn. Naturally, for some time afterwards food companies were cautious about launching new GM food products.

THAT'S AMAZING!

At about the same time as the Flavr Savr tomato was launched, some scientists were thinking of trying to put the genes of an Arctic fish in plants. The Arctic flounder survives in icy waters because its body makes an oil that stops the water in its body freezing. Some scientists thought that if they could put this "anti-freeze gene" in plants, they might survive frosts better. It was only an idea, but newspapers mixed the story up with the Flavr Savr tomato. The myth soon spread that scientists were trying to put fish genes in tomatoes. People even began to think that the tomatoes would taste fishy!

This simplified diagram shows how a flounder gene could one day be used to produce a frost-resistant tomato.

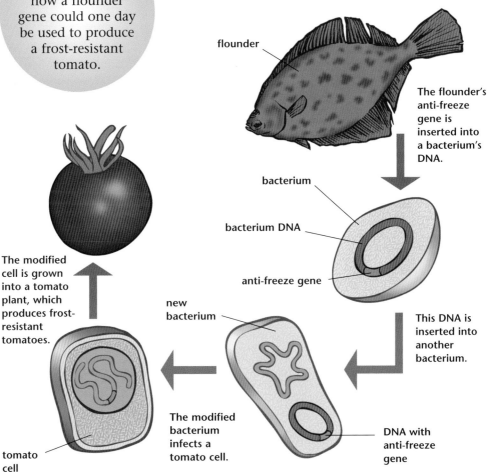

flounder

The flounder's anti-freeze gene is inserted into a bacterium's DNA.

bacterium

bacterium DNA

anti-freeze gene

This DNA is inserted into another bacterium.

The modified cell is grown into a tomato plant, which produces frost-resistant tomatoes.

new bacterium

DNA with anti-freeze gene

The modified bacterium infects a tomato cell.

tomato cell

Better foods

For many scientists, playing around with GM foods is a temptation that is too exciting to resist. For the moment they are holding off on the weirder ideas, such as chocolate-flavoured spinach! But they are working on a number of others.

For instance, many people drink decaffeinated coffee. Caffeine is the substance in coffee that wakes you up and makes you feel more alert. But too much caffeine can make people anxious, and may cause heart problems in the long term. Decaffeinated coffee has its caffeine removed during processing. Biotech scientists wondered whether the coffee beans themselves could be engineered to be caffeine-free.

In 2003, Japanese scientist Hiroshi Sano and his team created a decaffeinated coffee plant. Using a technique called RNA interference, they neutralized the gene that makes caffeine. RNA interference is the process that Calgene used to delay ripening in the Flavr Savr tomato. When a cell is ready to make a **protein**, it copies the right section of its DNA to make mRNA (see page 13). The mRNA then goes to make the protein, using the chemicals gathered by tRNA. RNA interference works by adding a back-to-front version of the gene. The back-to-front gene then interferes with the normal RNA and stops it working.

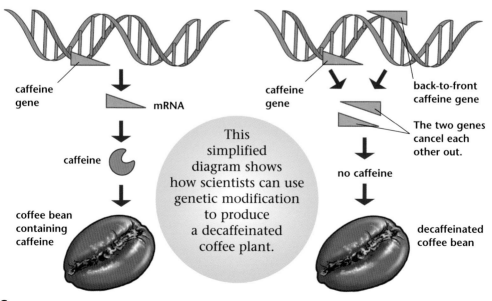

caffeine gene

mRNA

caffeine

coffee bean containing caffeine

caffeine gene

back-to-front caffeine gene

The two genes cancel each other out.

no caffeine

decaffeinated coffee bean

This simplified diagram shows how scientists can use genetic modification to produce a decaffeinated coffee plant.

No-cry onions

Another idea was to change onions so that they no longer make you cry. Often, people cutting onions find their eyes watering because of a stinging vapour released by the onion. Scientists had thought that this vapour was connected to the onion's flavour, so cutting out the vapour would make the onion tasteless. Then, in 2003, scientists at the House Foods Corporation, in Japan, found that the enzyme that makes people cry has nothing to do with the flavour. They have now located the gene that makes this enzyme. By neutralizing this gene, they believe they can produce onions that taste normal but do not make you cry.

Onions that give you flavour but no tears would be very popular with most cooks.

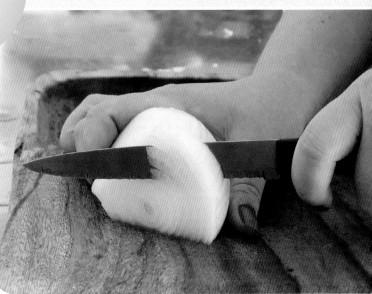

WHY DID BRITISH CUSTOMERS REJECT GM TOMATO PASTE?

One of the few GM foods sold in the United Kingdom was the Zeneca company's tomato paste. For this, the tomatoes were modified to make them last much longer than usual in paste form. Zeneca's paste was sold for a while in British supermarkets, such as Sainsbury's and Safeway's. But, by the late 1990s, people's worries over GM foods persuaded the supermarkets to stop selling the paste. No GM food has been sold in the United Kingdom since, but GM tomato paste is still widely sold in the United States.

Genetically modifying animals

Most of the early GM food breakthroughs involved plants. Scientists were also trying to modify the **genes** of farm animals, but this presented its own problems.

Once a plant's seeds had been modified, scientists could grow any number of GM plants. With animals, they could insert altered genes into cells grown in a **culture** solution in a laboratory. But it was a very different matter to produce an entire animal.

In the mid-1990s, Ian Wilmut and Keith Campbell led a team at the Roslin Institute, in Scotland, that finally solved the problem. All animals grow from eggs. However, with some animals, you cannot see the eggs because they develop inside the body. Wilmut and Campbell removed the genes from the eggs of sheep. They replaced them with genes taken from an adult sheep, which had been grown in a cell culture. They then placed the eggs with new genes in the womb of a female sheep. The eggs developed normally in the sheep's womb. Finally, the sheep gave birth to a lamb, which they called Dolly.

This photograph shows Dolly, the world's first sheep cloned from an adult sheep cell, at eight months old.

Dolly was the world's first animal cloned from an adult cell. An animal born in the normal way always has a mix of genes from its mother and father. This means that it has a mix of characteristics. However, clones are animals that develop directly from the **DNA** of a single animal. This means that a sheep clone is genetically identical to the sheep its genes come from.

Although Dolly was a clone, her genes were unmodified. In 1998, the biotech company PPL worked with the Roslin scientists to produce another sheep, which they called Polly. Like Dolly, Polly was a clone. The difference was that Polly's genes were modified. Her genes included a human gene that would enable Polly to produce a **protein** in her milk that made blood clot. This protein, called Factor IX, could be used to help treat people with a disease called haemophilia, which makes them bleed very easily.

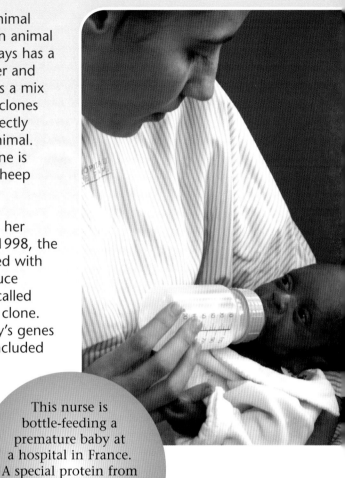

This nurse is bottle-feeding a premature baby at a hospital in France. A special protein from GM cows could help premature babies grow and develop.

HOW COULD GM COWS HELP BABIES?

In 1997, scientists created Rosie, the first GM dairy cow. They engineered Rosie and eight other cows to produce a human protein called alpha-lactalbumin. This protein is rich in the **amino acids** that newborn babies need to grow well. Alpha-lactalbumin is found in human milk, and most babies get it through breastfeeding. Babies who are born too early cannot breastfeed. But they could be fed with protein and milk from GM cows. The protein would be made in bulk, purified, and added to powdered milk.

Monster pigs

GM farm animals present rather more problems than GM plants. Most GM plants grow fairly well. Cloned and GM animals, however, can sometimes be born dead or deformed, or they may develop illnesses as they get older.

For instance, in 1985, scientists inserted genes for human growth **hormone** into a pig. This pig became known as the Beltsville pig. The animal grew so large and so fast that it quickly became crippled with a bone disease called arthritis. Later, Dolly the sheep, the first mammal to be cloned from an adult cell, died at the age of six, which is quite young for a sheep.

This is a salmon farm in the Western Isles of Scotland. The fish are bred in cages in inland waters and grown in sea pens. If GM salmon were ever put in pens like these, they might easily escape. They could then attack wild salmon, or mate with them.

Nevertheless, scientists think it is worth continuing their work with GM animals. In the late 1990s, they introduced human genes into sheep, goats, and cows. These genes meant that the animals produced substances in their milk that could be used to treat illnesses in humans. These animals are still at an experimental stage.

Fast-growing fish

Another idea was to make animals grow bigger or faster. After the disaster with the Beltsville pig, scientists were cautious about trying this with farm animals. However, some researchers decided that it was safe to experiment with fish.

In 2000, a Canadian company called Aqua Bounty added human growth hormone genes to salmon. These GM salmon can grow more than 10 times faster than normal salmon, and much bigger. Some people have predicted that they could grow up to 4 metres (13 feet) long.

Aqua Bounty has now applied for approval from various governments to market their fish, but many people are worried. It is impossible to keep these salmon in a tank because the growing fish are so hungry that they eat each other. However, if they are kept in fish farms some of them might escape. If these GM salmon got out into the wild, they could attack and eat the wild salmon. There are also concerns that they could mate with the wild salmon. The modified gene could then get into the genes of wild salmon, and cause all sorts of problems. For instance, wild salmon might grow so big that they would be unable to swim back to their breeding grounds.

Aqua Bounty has responded to these worries by ensuring that their GM salmon are all sterile. This means that they can never have offspring and pass on their modified genes. But not everyone is reassured.

THAT'S AMAZING!

Australian scientists thought they could make life easier for sheep farmers by producing a GM sheep that sheared itself. They engineered the sheep so that the wool included a skin growth hormone. This made all the wool fall out at the same time, once it reached a certain length. This certainly saved shearing. Unfortunately, the sheep suffered from severe sunburn when they lost their wool.

A woman receives a vaccination at a health clinic in Ghana. Vaccination programmes such as this one are expensive, and do not reach all those who need them.

Food as medicine

At present, most medicines are made in factories. In the future, however, GM technology could enable us to grow medicines on farms. This is called pharming, combining the word "pharmacy" with the word "farming".

All types of animals and plants could be genetically modified to make medicines. Sheep, goats, and cows have already been modified to make medicines in their milk. Other animals, such as pigs, could be engineered to grow **organs** for human **transplants**. Animals used for meat could be altered so that their meat contained important substances, such as vitamins.

In future, plants may be modified to provide edible vaccines. Vaccines prevent people catching diseases such as polio and smallpox. However, vaccines are expensive to make and store, and they have to be refrigerated. In addition, trained medical staff must give them. This means that not everyone gets the vaccinations they need – especially in poorer countries.

HOW DO VACCINES WORK?

Vaccines work by activating your body's own defences. A vaccine is a dead or harmless version of a germ. Nevertheless, your body's defences react to it, and produce chemicals called **antibodies**. Antibodies help your body fight particular germs and destroy them. Vaccination gives your body antibodies to fight the dead or harmless version of the germ. It is then armed and ready to fight the living germ, if it arrives.

In 1995, an American biotech scientist called Charles Arntzen wondered if vaccine genes could be put into food plants. If this could be done, vaccines could be grown locally in any quantity that was needed. Anyone eating the food grown on these plants would be automatically protected against disease.

For scientists developing edible vaccines, the disease that is highest on the list is diarrhoea. For most people in developed countries, diarrhoea is just an unpleasant stomach upset. But for people in poor countries, it is often combined with a lack of water. If this happens, it can be fatal. Each year, about 3 million babies die from diarrhoea.

Our bodies recognize a germ by proteins, called **antigens**, on the germ's surface. To create an edible vaccine for diarrhoea, scientists are trying to put the gene for the germ's antigen into food plants. To do this, they first insert the diarrhoea germ's antigen gene into the *Agrobacterium tumefaciens* **bacteria**, using **plasmids** (see pages 24–25). The bacteria deliver the modified gene into the plant's cells. The plant cells multiply in a **gall**, which eventually sprouts its own roots. This is then put into the soil, and should grow into a plant.

This Ugandan boy is carrying some recently harvested bananas. Bananas and potatoes are cheap and widely grown. Scientists have therefore considered using them for edible vaccines.

GM foods today and tomorrow

Scientists have come a long way since **DNA** was first discovered half a century ago. GM foods are now a reality. Soya beans, for instance, are used as an ingredient in two-thirds of all processed food – and most soya is now GM (see pages 32 and 33). Experts think that up to 60 per cent of all processed food on supermarket shelves throughout the world contains GM soya.

GM foods offer many benefits. Crops can be made to grow bigger and quicker, with added **protein** and vitamins. They could be made to grow in extreme weather and soil conditions. They can be made resistant to pests or weedkillers. Extra benefits, such as longer shelf life, can be added to foods. GM foods and farm produce could solve many of the world's food and health problems, allowing good food to be grown quickly, with all the right nutrients to keep people healthy.

But there are many critics of GM food technology. GM crops are grown widely in the United States and several other countries. Yet they are mostly banned in Europe. Many people are worried about eating GM food products. They fear that these foods could cause allergies or other health problems. Environmentalists are worried that GM crops could spread modified genes into other plants and animals. If this happens, they say, there is no way of knowing what the long-term effects would be.

TALKING SCIENCE

"*I happen to believe that this kind of genetic modification takes mankind into realms that belong to God, and to God alone. Apart from certain highly beneficial and specific medical applications, do we have the right to experiment with, and commercialise, the building blocks of life? [...] We simply do not know the long-term consequences for human health and the wider environment of releasing plants bred in this way...*"
Prince Charles, *Daily Telegraph* newspaper, United Kingdom, 1998

To see whether such fears are justified, some governments in Europe have set up trials. The idea is to grow GM crops in a controlled way on a real farm, and then watch what happens. Trials like this have been going on for a number of years, but the results have been controversial. Some scientists say they show that GM technology is completely safe. Others say they show the opposite.

Whatever the truth, the discovery of DNA and GM food has been one of the most extraordinary scientific stories of our time. Scientists now have the power to change the very nature of life itself. The question people are asking is: should they do so?

Activists destroyed this test site for genetically modified maize in south-west France, in 2001. Campaigners had forced the French government to publish a list of districts where **genetically engineered** plants were being tested.

Timeline

1869 Friedrich Miescher discovers nuclein, later called DNA.

1928 Frederick Griffith discovers how the danger of one type of pneumonia can be transferred to harmless bacteria.

1944 Oswald Avery finds that the transforming factor is DNA.

1952 Rosalind Franklin uses X-rays to photograph the DNA molecule.

1953 James Watson and Francis Crick discover the double helix shape of the DNA molecule.

1961 Francis Crick, Sidney Brenner, and other scientists discover messenger RNA.

1961 Crick and Brenner show that the DNA code is based on groups of three bases.

1961 Marshall Nirenberg discovers the code for a particular amino acid.

1966 Nirenberg, Gobind Khorana, and Robert Holley work out the complete genetic code.

1967 Arthur Kornberg uses ligase as DNA glue, to produce the first artificial life.

1968 Werner Arber discovers restriction enzymes, which work like DNA scissors.

1971 Stanley Cohen discovers how to use plasmids to insert genes into bacteria.

1972 Paul Berg makes the first recombinant DNA molecule.

1973 Cohen and Boyer make the first genetically modified organism (GMO) using recombinant DNA.

1975 "Pandora's Box Conference" is held at Asilomar, California, United States

1977 Fred Sanger discovers DNA sequencing.

1978 Genentech markets the first GM product, human insulin.

1980 The first GM mouse is produced.

1983 The first GM crop, tobacco, is produced.

1985 GM human growth hormone goes on sale.

1985 The first GM farm animal, the Beltsville pig, is produced.

1986 Discovery of how *Agrobacteria tumefaciens* could be used to insert modified genes into plants.

1987 Gene gun, for inserting modified genes into plants, is invented by John Sanford.

1990 Electroporation technique, for inserting modified genes into plants, is invented.

1994 First insect-repelling *Bacillus thuringiensis* toxin (Bt) cotton plant is grown.

1994 Calgene markets the Flavr Savr tomato, the first GM food.

1996 First Roundup Ready® soya beans are planted.

1996 Team led by Ian Wilmut and Keith Campbell produces Dolly, the first animal cloned from an adult cell.

1997 Biotech company PPL, Ian Wilmut, and Keith Campbell produce Polly, the first cloned GM farmed animal.

1997 Rosie, the first GM milk cow, is produced.

1998 Monsanto produces the "Terminator gene".

1998 UK supermarkets ban GM products.

1999 Modified *Rhizobium* bacteria are released into soil to improve nitrogen fixing.

2000 Aqua Bounty produces giant GM salmon.

2000 Discovery of contamination by GM seeds of oilseed rape imported into the United Kingdom from Canada.

2002 Eduardo Blumwald and Hong-Xia Zhang produce a salt-tolerant tomato plant.

2003 Scientists produce "golden rice" with added beta-carotene to give people extra vitamin A.

2003 Indian scientists produce a high-protein potato.

2003 Hiroshi Sano creates a decaffeinated coffee plant.

2004 Unmodified crops are shown to be contaminated by GM crops in many countries.

2005 GM trials for Britain's winter oilseed rape crop show that wildlife and the environment would suffer if the GM crop were grown in the United Kingdom.

Biographies

These are some of the leading scientists in the story of DNA and GM food.

Oswald Avery (1877–1955)

Oswald Avery was born in Nova Scotia, Canada, but spent most of his working life at the Rockefeller Institute, New York, in the United States. Avery worked there as one of the first biologists who studied the DNA molecule. In 1944, Avery discovered that DNA carried genes. He made this great breakthrough with an experiment. Avery's experiment showed that DNA was the substance that could transform a harmless bacterium into a dangerous one. Despite his important discovery, he never received a Nobel Prize.

Herbert Boyer

Born in Pennsylvania, in the United States, Herbert Boyer became a research biologist at the University of California. There, he did pioneering work on restriction enzymes, the proteins known as "DNA scissors". In 1973, he teamed up with Stanley Cohen. Together, they produced the world's first recombinant DNA organism. Boyer went on to found the first biotech company, Genentech, in 1976. Genentech made the first GM product to be sold, human insulin, in 1978.

Stanley Cohen

Born in Brooklyn, New York, Stanley Cohen was educated at the University of Michigan, in the United States. In the 1950s, he discovered growth factors with biologist Rita Levi-Montalcini. He and Levi-Montalcini were later awarded the Nobel Prize for Physiology for this discovery. However, his most famous work came in the early 1970s when he was researching at Stanford University, in the United States. There, he discovered how plasmids could take genetic material into bacterial cells. Then, in 1973, he produced the first recombinant DNA organism with Herbert Boyer.

Francis Crick (1916–2004)

British physicist Francis Crick, together with James Watson, discovered the double spiral shape of the DNA molecule in 1953. Crick was born in Northamptonshire, in the United Kingdom, in 1916. He earned his degree at University College, London. But it was at Cambridge University that he did most of his important work. After discovering the structure of DNA with Watson, he went on to play a key part in finding out the role of messenger RNA in cells. He also laid the groundwork for breaking the genetic code.

Rosalind Franklin (1920–1958)

Rosalind Franklin was a scientist who studied the structure of crystals. Her work proved vital to Watson and Crick's discovery of the double spiral shape of DNA. She was born in London and gained her degree at Cambridge. In 1951, she went to work at King's College, London. There, she began to study the DNA molecule, using X-rays. Without her knowing it, Watson looked at Franklin's photographs. They gave him vital clues to the shape of DNA. Crick said that Franklin would have worked out the structure of DNA in three months if he and Watson had not got there first. She died of cancer in 1958.

Friedrich Miescher (1844–1895)

Miescher was a Swiss-German biologist, born in Basel, Switzerland. As a student, he discovered nuclein, the substance that later came to be known as DNA. He made his great discovery while he was a student at the University of Tübingen, Germany. Research on nuclein remained central to his work. He made the first pure extract of DNA from the cells of salmon sperm in the 1870s. Towards the end of his life, he began to consider how heredity might be controlled by the structure of the DNA molecule.

James Watson

Born in Chicago, in the United States, James Watson went to the United Kingdom in 1951 to work at the Cavendish Laboratory in Cambridge. There, he teamed up with Francis Crick. Together, they worked out that the DNA molecule is shaped like a double spiral. In 1988, Watson became head of the Human Genome Project, the project to map all the genes in human DNA. He left the project in 1992. Watson is known for his controversial views. He is a strong supporter of GM crops. He thinks their benefits far outweigh the possible environmental risks.

Ian Wilmut

Born in the United Kingdom, Wilmut studied genetic engineering at Cambridge University. In 1974, he moved to the Roslin Institute in Edinburgh, Scotland. There, he and cell biologist Keith Campbell led the team that produced Dolly, the world's first sheep cloned from an adult cell, in 1996. Wilmut, Campbell, and their team went on to produce Polly, the world's first genetically modified cloned sheep, in 1997.

Glossary

amino acid one of the 20 or so basic chemicals of life. Proteins are built up from different combinations of amino acids.

antibody protein in an animal's body that targets invading substances

antigen identification mark on the surface of a germ that invades an animal's body

bacterium microscopically small living thing made of just one cell. Unlike other living cells, bacteria cells have no nucleus. Some are disease-causing germs but most are harmless.

base one of the four chemicals that DNA and RNA use, like letters, to make up the code for building different proteins

chromosome microscopically small bundle containing some of a cell's DNA. Human cells have 22 matching pairs of chromosomes. The 23rd pair is XY for men, and XX for women.

codon one of the groups of three base "letters" in the genetic code that make up a single "word". Each "word" is the code for a particular amino acid.

culture mixture of nutrients used for growing tiny organisms, such as bacteria, in a laboratory

DNA (deoxyribonucleic acid) chemical, found in every living cell, that carries all the cell's basic life instructions

electroporation introducing new genes into plant pollen by using electricity to open up pores in the pollen grains

element one of the 100 or so basic substances, such as oxygen and carbon, that make up all other substances

enzyme special type of protein that triggers or speeds up chemical reactions in living things

fertilizer natural or chemical substance that is put on the land to make crops grow better

flavonoid yellowish substance that occurs naturally in many plants. Flavonoids made in the roots of some plants attract *Agrobacteria*.

gall cancer-like growth on a plant

gene basic unit of heredity, which codes for a particular protein

genetic code chemical code used by DNA and RNA to instruct the cell to make particular proteins

genetic engineering process in which scientists alter a living thing's genes

germination when a seed or pollen starts to grow

heredity passing on of characteristics from generation to generation

hormone chemical released in the body to trigger particular processes

larva insect at an early stage of its life, when it may look like a worm or a caterpillar

legume plant, such as a pea or a bean, that has pods

molecule smallest naturally occurring particle of a chemical, made up of one or more atoms

nodule tiny swelling on the roots of plants, especially legumes. They are formed by bacteria that help plants get nitrogen from the soil.

nucleic acid complex chemical found in living cells. DNA and RNA are nucleic acids.

nucleus control centre of a living cell

organ complex part of the body, such as the liver or kidney, that has a particular role in the body

organism any living thing

pesticide chemical designed to kill pests, such as certain insects, that damage crops or garden plants

phosphate combination of substances made from phosphorus. Phosphates play a key role in DNA.

plasmid small ring of DNA found in bacteria

pollen tiny, dust-like particles that carry a plant's male sex cells

pore tiny hole in an animal's skin, or the surface of a plant, that lets substances in and out

protein one of the complex chemicals that make up all living things

recombinant DNA piece of DNA from one living thing added to the DNA of another

replication process by which DNA copies itself

ribosome part of the cell where RNA assembles amino acids to make proteins

RNA one of the two main nucleic acids. RNA is like DNA but has only one strand, not two. RNA makes proteins directly.

species particular type of living thing, such as a lion or a gorilla, that has similar offspring

stamen one of the male parts of a flower, which carries pollen

staple food that is needed all the time because it makes up the main part of a diet

stigma one of the female parts of a flower, which holds the eggs

strain type of living thing, e.g. bacteria

transplant organ or tissue that is moved from one part of the body to another, or from one person to another

vacuole large storage area, inside a plant cell, that holds sap

virus disease-causing microbe that is many times smaller than a bacterium

white blood cell pale-coloured, cell in the blood that plays an important role in the body's defence system

Further resources

If you have enjoyed this book and want to find out more, you can look at the following books and websites.

Books

21st Century Debates: Food Supply
Rob Bowden
(Hodder Wayland, 2002)

Discovery of DNA
Camille de la Bedoyere
(Evans Brothers, 2005)

Genes and DNA
Richard Walker
(Kingfisher, 2003)

Genetic Engineering
Anne Rooney
(Chrysalis Books, 2003)

Genetics: The Study of Heredity
J. Mahoney
(Ticktock Media, 2005)

Internet-linked Introduction to Genes and DNA
Anna Claybourne
(Usborne, 2003)

Saving our World:
Genetically Modified Food
Nigel Hawkes
(Aladdin, 2000)

Websites

Gene Technology Access Centre
www.genecrc.org/site/ko/
index_ko.htm
A simple and very informative site about genetics set up by the Gene Technology Access Centre.

Genetically modified crops
www.geocities.com/gm_crops
Award-winning Australian site where people exchange views on GM food, with links to other sites about GM food.

GlaxoSmithKline
www.genetics.gsk.com/kids/
dna01.htm
A fun site about genetics and DNA, featuring the cartoon character Professor U.Gene, with various learning activities. It is sponsored by the pharmaceutical company GlaxoSmithKline.

Index

Index

Titles in the *Chain Reactions* series include:

Hardback   0 431 18593 X

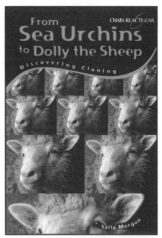

Hardback   0 431 18594 8

Hardback   0 431 18595 6

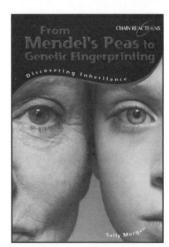

Hardback   0 431 18596 4

Hardback   0 431 18597 2

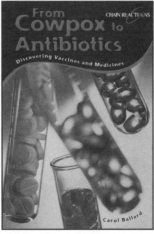

Hardback   0 431 18598 0

Find out about other titles from Heinemann Library on our website www.heinemann.co.uk/library